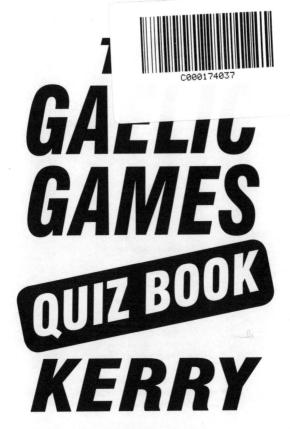

THE
GAELIC
GAMES

QUIZ BOOK

KERRY

ANDY
WATTERS

The
History
Press
Ireland

Thanks to my dad Frank, a lifelong GAA fan,
for his help with the questions in this book

First published 2014

The History Press Ireland
50 City Quay
Dublin 2
Ireland

www.thehistorypress.ie

British Library Cataloguing in Publication Data.
A catalogue record for this book is available from the British Library.

ISBN 978 1 84588 851 0

Typesetting and origination by The History Press

Contents

Introduction

Kerry is known as 'the Kingdom'. The county colours inspire confidence in the men and women who wear them and fear in opponents from their first glimpse of that green and gold jersey which has become synonymous with attacking élan, flair, style and success in Gaelic games.

The games, particularly Gaelic football, are a religion in the county and pious Kerrymen have won more All-Ireland senior football titles than any other county.

For some of the best players ever to lace up boots – from Joe Keohane, Mick O'Connell, Mick O'Dwyer, Páidí Ó Sé, Pat Spillane to Colm Cooper – playing for Kerry has been life's greatest honour, a privilege and a labour of love.

The prominence of Gaelic football in the county today can be attributed to local traditions in the game of 'Caid' long before the establishment of the Gaelic Athletic Association (GAA), but Kerry's first national title was actually in the game of hurling – in 1891.

The county's initial All-Ireland football title wasn't captured until 1903, almost twenty years after the GAA was founded, but since then thirty-five more have been won and Kerry's women have also enjoyed success in ladies' football.

In its formative years, Gaelic games were locked in a power struggle with rugby, which threatened to become the dominant sport in the county.

Rugby was popular and widespread but in October 1888, the influential Laune Rangers club in Killorglin held a meeting at which their captain J.P. O'Sullivan called on members to concentrate instead on Gaelic football.

Kerry's first annual GAA Convention was held in Tralee in November 1888, at which nineteen clubs were represented and a Kerry county board was formed.

In 1889, the inaugural county championships were held, and Kerry, represented by Laune Rangers, made its first appearance in the Munster championship.

A decade later, however, and the game had regressed to the point of extinction – no county conventions were held in 1898 or 1899 and rugby, the 'garrison game', reclaimed some of the ground it had lost.

Compelled by what he saw as the erosion of his national identity, the emergence of the energetic Thomas F. O'Sullivan helped galvanise Gaels in the county and a new county board was formed in 1900.

O'Sullivan, a journalist, was fervently opposed to what he perceived as the pollution of Irish culture by British sports and embarked on a crusade to undermine those involved in playing rugby while at the same time promoting Gaelic games.

The introduction of 'the Ban' or Rule 27 in 1902 which forbade GAA members from engaging or promoting 'foreign' sports dealt rugby a knockout blow and Gaelic football assumed the dominance it has held ever since.

In 1902, Kerry reached their first All-Ireland final. Though they lost to Tipperary, they made the final again the following year and won it for the first time.

Kerry, captained by the legendary Austin Stack, who would later take part in the 1916 Easter Rising and after whom one of Tralee's clubs is named, retained the All-Ireland title in 1904.

Steady progress continued and the first of two four-in-a-rows began in 1929 when the Kingdom beat Kildare 1-8 to 1-5. John Joe Sheehy top scored with 6 points as Kerry defended their title and John Joe Landers's 2 goals saw off Monaghan the following year.

The fourth title of the run arrived in 1931. Again Kildare were the opposition and this time Austin Stack's clubman Jackie Ryan led the way with 6 points.

Kerry dominance secured their reputation as Gaelic football's powerhouse and since then successive generations have been inspired by the feats of their forebears – young men driven on by tales of the great deeds performed by the men who went before them.

Kerry won two more All-Irelands in the 1930s, three in the 1940s and three more in the 1950s when Mick O'Connell emerged as the team's midfield star.

Galway and Down were formidable rivals in the 1960s, but Kerry won All-Irelands in 1962 (the last of eight under the management of Dr Eamon O'Sullivan) and 1969 and, as the 1970s dawned in glorious technicolor, marauding Kerry teams decked out in green and gold became engrained in popular culture.

Beating Meath in 1970 secured a twenty-second All-Ireland for the Kingdom and the twenty-third came five years later, the first under the management of the legendary Mick O'Dwyer. 'Micko' was still at the helm when they won again in 1978 – the start of another four-in-a-row.

Eoin 'Bomber' Liston and Mikey Sheehy ran riot as Dublin were routed, and Sheehy weighed in with 2-6 the following year as the Dubs were once again put to the sword.

Kerry, with Sheehy, Liston, Jack O'Shea, 'Ogie' Moran, Pat Spillane and others in their pomp, continued to dominate in the 1980s and they took the first title of the new decade by beating Roscommon.

They won again in 1981, this time against Offaly, to equal the record set half-a-century earlier and the talk throughout 1982 was of a ground-breaking 'five-in-a-row'. But, against the odds, Offaly avenged their defeat the previous year to spoil the party with a dramatic one-point win.

Despite that disappointment, Kerry recorded a treble between 1984 and 1986 but the good times ended there and the Kingdom suffered the longest drought in its rich history, going eleven years without a title.

The drought ended in 1997 when a Maurice Fitzgerald-inspired Kingdom team beat Mayo. Showing an impeccable sense of timing, Kerry were the first All-Ireland champions of this millennium.

With a new batch of stars, including the Ó Sé brothers and Colm Cooper coming to the fore, Kerry lifted the Sam Maguire Cup five times in the decade, despite increasing competition from their rivals.

From obscure trivia to the essential facts you need to know, what follows are thirty-five themed rounds of questions designed to entertain and amuse – so get your thinking caps on – it's quiz time!

A Mixed Grill

Of the thirty-five rounds of questions in this book, thirty-three are related to specific topics or have related themes. But before you get on to those it's probably advisable to warm-up with a general knowledge round.

1. Which legendary Kerry player was actually a Corkman, born in Fermoy?

2. Which Kerry footballer won Sigerson Cups with both University College Cork and Tralee IT?

3. What was the final score when Offaly denied Kerry five-in-a-row in the 1982 All-Ireland final?

4. That was the second occasion on which Kerry went into a decider hoping to seal a fifth consecutive All-Ireland title only to be thwarted in the final. The first time was in 1933. Who beat them then?

5. Of which Kerry club is Paul Galvin a member?

6. Which Austin Stack's clubman played at centre full-back for Kerry in five consecutive All-Ireland finals from 1978 to 1982?

7. Who published *The Art and Science of Gaelic Football* in 1958?

8. Which Kerry player wrote *Shooting from the Hip*?

9. Kerry scored 2 goals in the 2005 All-Ireland final. Name either goalscorer.

10. Which Kerry forward was voted 'Footballer of the Year' in 2006?

Round

2

Family Ties

In Kerry success does, literally, breed success. Fathers and sons, grandfathers and grandsons, brothers, nephews and uncles have all worn the green and gold jersey with distinction across generations. This section is all about family ties.

1. The Spillane brothers of the Templenoe club all followed in the footsteps of their father Tom into the Kerry senior team. Can you name the three of them?

2. How many All-Ireland medals did they win altogether and how many did each win?

3. The brothers won three All-Ireland titles together. In which years?

4. In doing so they equalled the extraordinary achievements of the Landers brothers in the 1930s and the Sheehy brothers in the 1960s. Another set of three brothers have played on an All-Ireland-winning team since then. Name them.

5. Denis Curran won an All-Ireland medal with Kerry in 1903 – his great-grand-nephew did the same a century later. Who is he?

6. Who were the twin brothers that played against Kerry in the 2002 All-Ireland final?

7. Liam Hassett captained Kerry in the 1997 All-Ireland win but he wasn't captain in the Munster final win over Clare earlier that year. Who captained the Kingdom in that game?

8. Which player, who played for Kerry in 1992–93, switched counties and in 1998 won an Allstar for his performances with Kildare who were managed by his father, a former Kerry manager and player?

9. Who are the only Kerry father and son to captain All-Ireland senior football winners?

10. John Dowling captained Kerry to the Sam Maguire in 1955. His grandson is a star of the current side. Can you name him?

AKA
(Also Known As)

With many players linked by common surnames, and even first names, nicknames have often been used to tell players apart. Sometimes players have earned their moniker through their deeds on the pitch. Can you identify famous players and their nicknames?

1. Who is known as 'the Bomber'?

2. Whose nickname is 'Star'?

3. Colm Cooper is better known as …

4. How did he get that nickname?

5. Paddy Brosnan won three All-Irelands with Kerry during a career that lasted from 1938 to 1952. What is his nickname?

6. Who answers to 'Pony'?

7. 'Ogie' Moran was a star of the Kerry teams of the 1980s. What is his actual Christian name?

8. What was the late Tim Kennelly's nickname?

9. Which Finuge star is also known as 'Rocky'?

10. Which midfielder had the nickname 'Panda'?

Micko

One of Kerry's greatest strengths through the years has been their unity of purpose on the field. But within that ethos the county has produced many of the most outstanding players, managers and characters the game has ever seen. Mick O'Dwyer was all three rolled into one – a terrific player, an astute mentor and a one-off personality. This section is devoted to the legendary 'Micko'.

1. Where was Mick O'Dwyer born?

2. When did he make his championship debut for Kerry?

3. He holds the record for the biggest individual scoring haul. What is it?

4. How many championship games did he play for Kerry?

5. His biggest scoring haul in a championship match was
   1-6 and he managed the feat twice – against the same
   county. Can you name it?

6. How many All-Ireland titles did he win as a player?

7. He took over as Kerry manager in which year and
   when did he step down?

8. How many Sam Maguire Cups did he win as manager
   of the Kingdom?

9. How many other counties did he manage?

10. O'Dwyer has guided teams to victory against every
    one of Ireland's thirty two counties (including Kerry).
    Against which team did he complete this unique
    managerial feat?

Grounds for Optimism

You're always assured a warm welcome and a tough game when you arrive at any ground in Kerry. Like the rest of the country, there was a time when the cows had to be cleared off the pitch before the game could start, but thankfully that's history now and the questions in this section are all related to Kerry's GAA grounds.

1. Can you name Kerry's two county grounds?

2. Which is bigger and what is its capacity?

3. When did Austin Stack Park last host a Kerry game?

4. At which stadium did Kerry lose the All-Ireland final of 1947?

5. Which club play at Tom Healy Park?

6. Name the ground which is home to Listowel Emmet's?

7. Kerry reached their first All-Ireland final in 1892 – where was it played?

8. Where did Kerry meet Kildare in the 1905 All-Ireland final?

9. Which club's home is Dromore Sportsfield?

10. Beale GAC play home games at Stack Park. Where did the ground get its name?

Round

6

Páidí

The world of GAA was stunned by the untimely death of the great Páidí Ó Sé in 2012 at the age of 57. Páidí was a genuine legend of the game – as a player and a manager and one of Gaelic football's outstanding characters.

1. Where was he born?

2. What age did he make his senior debut for An Ghaeltacht?

3. In which season did Páidí make his senior inter-county debut?

4. How many Munster championships did he win?

5. How many All-Irelands?

6. In the 1982 All-Ireland final, Páidí scored 2 points in a losing cause. Which county won the game?

7. Páidí's first, and last, championship games were against the same county. Can you name it?

8. How many Allstar awards did Páidí receive?

9. How many All-Ireland titles did Kerry win with O Se as manager?

10. One of his greatest achievements outside his native Kerry was winning the Leinster championship while manager of an unfashionable county. Name it.

The Swinging Sixties

Anew force from the north emerged as a major player in this decade, while a giant from Connacht also made its presence felt. Kerry challenged every year, but things didn't always go their way.

1. How many All-Ireland finals did Kerry reach in the decade?

2. Kerry didn't concede a goal on the way to the All-Ireland final in 1960. Who did they play in the decider at Croke Park?

3. Who was the top-scorer for Kerry that day with 4 points? It was his final championship game for the Kingdom.

4. Kerry were beaten semi-finalists in 1961. Who provided the opposition?

5. The losing run ended in 1962, when Kerry beat Roscommon in the final. Who top-scored with 8 points from midfield?

6. Valentia great O'Connell scored 7 points in the All-Ireland semi-final the following year, but Kerry lost the game. Who to?

7. The sides met again in the 1964 decider. Which county emerged victorious?

8. Cork extinguished Kerry hopes in the 1966 Munster final with a 2-7 to 1-7 win. Which Ballyduff clubman scored Kerry's goal?

9. Down had the upper hand on Kerry once again in the 1968 All-Ireland final, but the Kingdom did win the final All-Ireland of the decade. Which Leinster county did they beat?

10. How many goals were scored in the game?

A League of Their Own

What better way to prepare for Croke Park in September than a trip to Ballybofey in February? The Sam Maguire Cup is the one that players and fans covet most, but the grounding board for all footballers is the league which is played in the spring. The following section relates to Kerry's achievements in the National Football League (NFL).

1. How many NFL titles have Kerry won?

2. When did the county win its first title?

3. Who were the opposition?

4. Kerry won four NFL titles between 1971 and 1974. Is that a record? And who holds the record?

5. Who top-scored with 0-7 in the 1974 NFL final replay win over Roscommon?

6. Kerry drew the 1969 NFL 'final'. Who were their opponents?

7. Kerry's biggest margin of victory was 29 points in 1992. Who were their unlucky opponents that day?

8. Which county inflicted Kerry heaviest league defeat?

9. What was Kerry's score in that game?

10. Kerry drew with Galway 1-8 to 0-11 in an NFL game on 3 March 1974. What is significant about the game?

That Winning Feeling

All Kerry fans and players keep their diary free for the third Sunday in September – just in case the Kingdom make one of their regular appearances in the All-Ireland final at Croke Park. The following section deals with some of Kerry's greatest glories.

1. What year did Kerry win its first All-Ireland title?

2. How many All-Ireland titles have Kerry won?

3. Kerry won a record five All-Ireland titles in the 1930s. In how many other decades have they matched that feat?

4. What was unique about Kerry's win in the 1914 All-Ireland final?

5. Five Kerry footballers have won eight All-Ireland titles. Can you name them?

6. Kerry's biggest total in an All-Ireland final is 4-15. Against whom and what year?

7. Who top-scored that day?

8. Who scored a hat-trick (three goals) in the 5-11 to 0-9 win over Dublin in 1978?

9. Not all of Kerry's final wins have been convincing. On how many occasions has a single point been the difference between the sides at the final whistle?

10. Who managed Kerry to the 2006 All-Ireland title?

You Can't Win Them All

Kerry put up with disappointments on a few occasions when other counties 'borrowed' the Sam Maguire Cup. Kerry fans never worry too much though – the cup never stays away for long – and this section recalls the occasions when Kerry have fallen just short of winning.

1. In how many All-Ireland finals have Kerry finished runners-up?

2. When did the county suffer its first defeat in an All-Ireland final?

3. In only one decade since have Kerry failed to make it to the Sam Maguire decider. Which one?

4. Kerry went into the 1982 All-Ireland final chasing a record five-in-a-row. Whose goal frustrated their efforts?

5. The Kingdom suffered back-to-back final defeats in the mid-1960s. Who won those games?

6. The biggest margin of defeat in a final was in 1972. What was it?

7. Who were the winners in 1972?

8. Down beat Kerry in the 1960 All-Ireland final. What was notable about the final pairing?

9. Who top-scored for Kerry that day?

10. Who beat Kerry in the famous Polo Grounds final of 1947?

The Munster Mash

Before the advent of the qualifier system in 2001, winning the Munster championship was a prerequisite on the way to All-Ireland success. Kerry have given their supporters some of the finest memories during their clashes with arch-rivals Cork for provincial honours.

1. How many Munster titles have Kerry won?

2. Their first win came in 1892. Who were the opposition?

3. Kerry has completed eight-in-a-row twice. The first was between 1958 and 1965. When was the second?

4. What is notable about the 1975 Munster championship win?

5. Who scored 2-10 in a Munster quarter-final against Limerick in 1995?

6. Kerry's biggest win in a Munster championship final came in 1932. Who were their opponents?

7. Who inflicted Kerry's biggest final loss?

8. Who top-scored in the 3-15 to 0-8 win over Clare in 2000?

9. Tony Barrett scored a point in the 1964 Munster final against Cork. Why was his contribution so memorable?

10. Kerry and Cork are Munster's 'Old Firm'. What is their longest sequence of final meetings?

Through the Back Door

Before 2001 Kerry might have played as few as four games on their way to the All-Ireland title. All that changed with the 'back door' which challenged the eventual champions with more games and offered provincial losers a second chance.

1. What was Kerry's first year in the qualifiers?

2. How many times have Kerry made it to the All-Ireland final via the qualifiers?

3. How many of those finals did they win?

4. How many did they lose?

5. Kerry lost to Donegal in the All-Ireland quarter-final in 2012. What was notable about the game?

6. Kerry's biggest win in the qualifiers was by 23 points in 2002. Who were their opponents?

7. What was notable about the game?

8. Who came on as a substitute for Colm Cooper that day, scored 2 points but never appeared for Kerry in the championship again?

9. What was notable about Kerry's All-Ireland final win in 2006?

10. Which legendary defender and former captain retired after the game?

Allstar
State of Mind

The Allstars are awarded annually to the fifteen best
footballers from that year's championship. They are
awarded from goalkeeper to left corner-forward
and came into being in 1971. Unsurprisingly Kerry players
have featured prominently on Allstars night every year.

1. Since 1971, how many Allstar teams have NOT
    featured a Kerry player?

2. Who was Kerry's first Allstar winner?

3. How many Allstar winners have been Kerry players?

4. Maurice Fitzgerald was the only Kerry player
    on the 1988 team. Who was the county's sole
    representative on the 1996 Allstar select?

5. Between 1988 and 1996, Kerry had one Allstar winner. Who was it?

6. Which Kerry player won most Allstar awards?

7. How many did he win?

8. Tim Kennelly won the second of his awards in 1980. In relation to that, what was significant about the 2009 Allstar team?

9. In which year did Kerry land their biggest haul of nine Allstars?

10. How many Allstars were awarded to Kerry footballers from 1990 to 1995?

The Seventies

The technicolour era had arrived and Kerry were the team to beat once again. Down and Galway faded, but new rivals emerged and Kerry fought out a thrilling series of duels at Headquarters.

1. How many All-Ireland titles did Kerry win in this decade?

2. Who made the last of his fifty-six championship appearances for the Kingdom as a substitute in the 1974 Munster final against Cork?

3. Kerry beat Meath in the All-Ireland final of 1970. The team posted formidable scores in all five of their championship outings – which was the lowest: 0-18, 1-17 or 0-23?

4. The 1972 All-Ireland final went to a replay. Who did Kerry take on?

5. Which opposition player scored 16 points over the two games?

6. Who made their debut at right half-forward in the 1975 win against Tipperary?

7. Kerry came through a Munster final replay against Cork to reach the 1976 All-Ireland final. Who won that year?

8. Kerry met Dublin in the 1978 final. What was their winning margin in the game?

9. Who was the top scorer with 3 goals and 2 points.

10. Kerry won back-to-back titles with another win the following year. Who were the opposition?

Round
15

Far Off Fields

Wearing that green and gold jersey is the ultimate for every Kerryman. But (apparently) man cannot live on GAA alone and Gaelic football has been the starting point from which several have gone on to, or were offered, careers in professional sports including soccer, rugby and Aussie Rules. Others have starred for Ireland in the hybrid 'International Rules series' against Australia.

1. Which multi-Sam Maguire Cup-winning forward was offered a trial by Southampton FC, but turned it down because he had to pay his own way?

2. Who won an All-Ireland medal in 1986 and then went on to win forty-one caps for Ireland at rugby?

3. Which Ireland and British and Irish Lions lock won an U21 Munster championship title with Kerry?

4. Darran O'Sullivan played at youth team level for which London soccer team?

5. Tadgh Kennelly won an All-Ireland with Kerry in 2009 before returning to which Aussie Rules side?

6. Which Scotland-born Kerry minor star played 150 games with Melbourne in the AFL?

7. Which well-known politician played club football with the Kerins O'Rahilly's and hurling with Crotta O'Neill's before representing Munster at rugby? (His father Dan won All-Irelands with Kerry in 1939 and 1940.)

8. This towering full-forward scored 4 points as Kerry won the Sam Maguire Cup in 2009 before leaving for St Kilda. Can you name him?

9. Which Kerry legend of the 1980s played for, and later assisted, manager Sean Boylan with, Ireland's International Rules side?

10. Who won basketball's National Cup and Superleague with the Tralee Tigers?

Round

16

Countdown

In this section answer questions from 10 down to 1 on a variety of topics.

1. Can you name the Spa clubman who played forty-three times for Kerry in league and championship and scored **10** goals?

2. In the 1947 Munster semi-final, Kerry scored a record **9** goals. Who were their unfortunate opponents?

3. In the 1970 Munster final against Cork, the Kerry left-corner forward scored **8** points. Who was he?

4. Which legendary Kerry goalie, won **seven** All-Ireland medals in the 1930s and '40s?

5. The captain of the 1980 All-Ireland winning team won a total of **six** Allstar Awards. Who was he?

6. Can you name the Laune Rangers forward who won **five** All-Ireland medals between 1997 and 2007?

7. Who wore the number **four** shirt (left corner-back) in the 1981 and 1982 finals?

8. **Three** brothers played together on **three** consecutive All-Ireland-winning sides. Who were they?

9. **Two** Kerry footballers were named at midfield in 'The Team of the Century' name them.

10. Only **one** player from St Patrick's, Blennerville has represented Kerry at senior level. Who is he?

Round

17

Who's Who?

1. Who holds the record for most senior championship appearances for Kerry?

2. Who wrote the first ever instruction manual entitled *How to Play Gaelic Football*?

3. Who, in 2003, became Kerry's first President of the GAA?

4. Who is Kerry's all-time leading scorer, having played 123 times in league and championship, and averaged 5 points per game?

5. Who was Kerry captain in millennium year 2000?

6. Who took over in the Kerry goal when Charlie Nelligan was sent off in the 1978 All-Ireland final against Dublin?

7. Who played for Kerry in an All-Ireland Final at the age of 17 in 1924, becoming the youngest ever winner of an All-Ireland medal?

8. Who did Jack O'Connor succeed as manager of the Kerry senior team in 2004?

9. Who was the Kerryman who refereed the All-Ireland finals of 1988 and 1994?

10. Who scored a hat-trick in the 1978 All-Ireland final when Kerry beat Dublin by 5-11 to 0-9?

Half Time

Interview with Colm Cooper

Colm Cooper, the Gaelic football superstar. Tall and lean with fiery ginger hair and a friendly grin, Kerry's captain is greeted at the door of St Paul's High School, Bessbrook by a row of fresh-faced pupils.

He shakes each by the hand with unassuming charm. 'Nice to meet you,' he says as he goes to the end of the row where school principal Jarlath Burns awaits with his arm also outstretched. 'The Gooch' greets the former Armagh captain with the same warmth he showed his students during his visit to the county Armagh school to promote his employer AIB/ First Trust's 'School Bank' initiative. He visits schools all around the country these days as part of his job, encouraging students with tips on business plans and savings. Back in his own school days he was the smallest lad in his class until he reached his mid-teens and added physical presence to the footballing talent already there.

Since then he has developed into the purest footballer of a generation with eyes in the back of his head, a dummy he's sold a thousand defenders, the goals, the points and, increasingly, a range of precision passing that can unlock the tightest defensive blanket.

Cooper is an accidental superstar – he doesn't feel he is one. When did the penny drop that he could be a star for Kerry? 'I'm not too sure has it dropped yet,' he says with a smile. 'But I suppose probably in second-level school from the age of 15 to 20 is where I made my biggest development as a footballer. 'I was always the smallest boy in the class so it took me a little while to catch up. But as I got older I got a little bit taller and stronger. My skill level was always at a decent high level but physically I was probably struggling a bit.

'As I got older my skill level was improving and then my strength started improving too; I was becoming a better player and more of an all-rounder of a player.'

Coming up through the ranks, his class was obvious but he struggled to make the Kerry teams because he lacked the physicality to compete with opponents and make his skills really count. 'At under-16 for Kerry I was only a sub on the team because I wasn't at the level other guys were in terms of physique and size,' he said.

'When I got to about 17 I made the Kerry minor panel fairly quickly and I was there for two years.

'I broke into the Kerry side then straight out of minor so I went from watching Kerry in the All-Ireland final in 2000 to actually playing in 2002 against Armagh. 'Things can happen so quickly and you don't get too much time to think; you just go with the flow. I'm lucky that I've just had a career that people dream of really in terms of having success – things have worked out really well for me.'

In Kerry's green and gold he has won four Sam Maguires and seven Munster titles, but national success with his club, Dr Croke's of Killarney, has proved more elusive. However, after several disappointments at club level he has another chance this year and is out of the Kingdom set-up at the minute to concentrate on an All-Ireland semi-final against Castlebar Mitchel's of Mayo on 15 February. 'We'll be taking them on at Portlaoise and it's going to be a tough match,' he said.

'We're down to the last four in Ireland now and all the teams are there on merit. We've come close the last couple of years and haven't performed in a couple of semi-finals which is bitterly disappointing, but we feel that we're a better team this year, we feel that we're more experienced and a little bit wiser.

'Time will tell on that but it's brilliant to be involved in the club championship. I always treat it as one of the toughest competitions in the country to win and it's been a dream of mine to win it.

'Our club did it in 1992 and I had two brothers playing. They won a medal so they have it over me a little bit on that score and I'm trying to catch up. If I get that medal I could keep them quiet for a little bit.'

Cooper admits he always keeps an eye on how old rivals Crossmaglen are getting on. The Armagh side had the wood on Croke's over the years – remember the 2012 semi-final that the Kerry champions led by 1-5 to a point but still managed to lose?

Cross exited the club championship after losing to Kilcoo, who in turn lost to Ballinderry, who will be Ulster's representatives in next month's semi-finals. 'Crossmaglen have been the benchmark for this competition for as long as I can remember, so you're always keeping an eye out for their results in Armagh and in Ulster,' he said. 'When they were gone it was big news of course but Ballinderry are coming out of Ulster and they are a fairly formidable team so I don't think it weakens the competition in any way that Crossmaglen are gone.

'Crossmaglen are a fantastic team and with the tradition they have people always keep an eye out for them, but the teams that are there at the moment are there on full merit.

'They may not be Crossmaglen, but I'm sure Castlebar will come with the same challenge and be a very, very hungry team.'

He's leaning towards St Vincent's, with Dublin stars Ger Brennan, Mossy Quinn, Diarmuid Connolly and others, in the other semi-final though he has been impressed with what he's seen of Martin McKinless's Ballinderry. 'I only know them from what I've seen on TV. I've just seen highlights and things, but they look to be a very organised team, very strong with a very good game-plan,' he said. 'They know what they're about. I suppose Vincent's will probably go into the game as slight favourites but that might play into Ballinderry's hands.

'I wouldn't be ruling them out for one second, I think they're an experienced team as well, they've been involved (in the All-Ireland club championships) before so they know how to win and they can grind it out.

'It's going to be a fascinating game and I think both semi-finals are too close to call.' When he does go back to the Kerry fold, either in mid-February or mid-March, he'll return to a team in transition under manager Eamonn

Fitzmaurice. 'If you go back to the 2009 team which won the All-Ireland, we've probably twelve to fourteen guys gone from that thrity which is nearly 50 per cent and that is a lot,' he said. 'We are in a transitional period – James O'Donoghue came in last year and Peter Crowley had a full season. Shane Enright had his first full season and we're just hoping that those guys can keep progressing and maybe one or two others put up their hand again to bring it on and give us older fellas a dig out. 'But last year was Eamonn's first year as Kerry manager as well so I'm sure he learned an awful lot. It's going to be a different season this year and we're looking for a little bit of progress. 'We got to the semi-final stage last year against Dublin – it was a great game but we just came out the wrong side of things. We're just hoping that we can go one better this year, get to the final and see what happens then.

'But that [the championship] is a long way off. We'll use the League for introducing new guys and hopefully that will stand to us going into the championship.'

The new players Kerry find will have some big boots to fill. Big names have hung up their boots and the Kingdom's right half-back berth is up for grabs for the first time in a decade-and-a-half after the retirement of the incomparable Tomás Ó Sé. 'Tomás has been an outstanding player for Kerry,' said Cooper.

'I played twelve years with him and when I go back it's going to be strange to go into the dressing room and not see him sitting in his spot. 'But look, that's the nature of football and it's the same in every county. No matter how many good or great players you have, time moves on and someone else comes in. 'I'm sure he'll miss it but he owes Kerry absolutely nothing. He's been one of the finest players in the country for a long, long time and we probably won't see another number five like him for years to come.'

Whether Kerry can unearth a new Tomás Ô Sé or not, Cooper feels that Dublin will be the team to beat once again this season.

'They're probably the stand-out team at the moment,' he said. 'But you're going to have teams who are going to come with a push again and, as All-Ireland champions, you can be knocked off your perch on any given day and I think you'll have the same contenders again this year – the Kerrys, the Tyrones …

'I think Donegal will come back with a push this year and you'll have a few teams who will find a bit of form during the League and put it up to them. 'I would put Dublin as favourites at the moment with a few coming in behind.'

Colm Cooper spoke to Andy Watters in February 2014. Sadly his hopes for Dr Croke's and his season with Kerry were destroyed by a cruciate ligament injury he suffered playing for his club in that All-Ireland Club Football Championship semi-final against Castlebar. 'The Gooch' will return in 2015.

Who, What, Where, When, Why ... ?

1. What distinctions do Martin Furlong of Offaly and Kerry's Declan O'Keefe have in common?

2. Who was the referee of the 2002 All-Ireland final when Armagh and Kerry met?

3. How many All-Ireland titles did Kerry win with Jack O'Connor as manager?

4. Who was voted 'Player of the Year' in 2004?

5. When Kerry won their first All-Ireland title in 1903, who were their opponents?

6. In what year did Kerry win the Sam Maguire Cup for the first time?

7. Top of the list of surnames on Kerry teams is 'O'Sullivan'. Thirty players called 'O'Sullivan' have played senior football for Kerry in league and championship over the years. Which surname comes second in the list?

8. Why did Louth have a 'walk-over' in the 1910 All-Ireland final?

9. Who was the manager of the Offaly team which beat Kerry in the 1982 All-Ireland final?

10. What experience do Kerry trio John O'Shea (1965), Charlie Nelligan (1975) and Páidí Ó Sé (1979) have in common?

Round

19

Numbers Game

Ten of the eleven numbers listed below are answers to one of the questions in this round. Keeping an eye out for the rogue number, can you match the correct number to answer each question? Pencil and paper needed.

6   8   4   75   10   23   56   7   9   14   36

What is, or was …

1. … the number of All-Ireland senior football finals in which Kerry have appeared?

2. … the number of Allstars won by Eoin Liston?

3. … the number of Kerry's Senior Football Munster titles?

4. ... the number of points scored by Maurice Fitzgerald in Kerry's 1997 All-Ireland final win over Mayo?

5. ... the number worn by Tom Spillane in the 1984 All-Ireland final?

6. ... the number of All-Ireland senior football finals involving Kerry that have gone to a replay?

7. ... the number of times Kerry have beaten Dublin in an All-Ireland Senior Football final?

8. ... the number of Kerry senior football All-Ireland wins?

9. ... the number of counties that Kerry have beaten at least once in All-Ireland senior football finals?

10. ... the number of All-Ireland senior football finals in which Mick O'Dwyer played?

Round
20

A Set of Clubs

K erry's footballing strength is built on a network of clubs from Sneem to Beale, where youngsters are introduced to the game and guided through the ranks from U6 to senior level. The following questions relate to Kerry's clubs.

1. Which Kerry club, formed in 1885, has won thirteen North Kerry senior football championships and plays at home in Frank Sheehy Park?

2. Can you name the club which won the Kerry county championship in 1911 but didn't win it again until 1989, a gap of seventy-eight years?

3. For which Killarney club does Colm Cooper play?

4. Five footballers from the Templenone club have represented Kerry at senior level in the championship and national league. What do they have in common?

5. Which West Kerry club appeared in four successive senior championship finals from 1999 to 2002, winning the senior championship for the first time in 2001?

6. Laune Rangers – with 12 wins – is the most successful club in Kerry senior championship finals. Which club, with 11 wins, comes second?

7. Which former Kerry club won nine county football championships between 1896 and 1919 as well as three county hurling championships in 1908, 1911 and 1912?

8. Which North Kerry Division One team's home ground is Jackie Finnerty Park?

9. Declan O'Sullivan and Aidan 'Shine' O'Sullivan who have, between them, represented Kerry 140 times in the senior championship and national league, are members of which club?

10. In which Kerry town is the Laune Rangers home ground, JP O'Sullivan Park?

The Eighties

Kerry began the decade as reigning All-Ireland champions after securing the titles of 1978 and 1979 and hoping to break new ground with an experienced group of talented players and a master tactician as manager.

1. How many championship games, including the All-Ireland final, did Kerry play in 1980?

2. The Kingdom made it three-in-a-row that year. Which county were beaten finalists?

3. Kerry beat Offaly in the semi-final. How many goals were scored in that extraordinary game?

4. Winning the following year meant Kerry had four Sam Maguires on-the-trot. Which county did they beat 1-12 to 0-8 in the final?

5. The following year Kerry chased an historic five in-a-row. Whose goal denied them?

6. Kerry had completed four-in-a-row between 1929 and 1932, what other county has managed that feat?

7. Kerry's youngest current club was formed in 1984. Name it?

8. Who was the club's first inter-county player?

9. Who captained Kerry to the 1984 All-Ireland title?

10. Kerry beat an Ulster county making its debut in the final in 1986. Name it?

Clubbing Together

For many Kerry clubs winning their divisional championship is the be-all and end-all, but after it there are the battles of the county championship. Some have gone on to dominate in Munster and then represent the province in the All-Ireland club championships.

1. Who won an All-Ireland club championship in 1992 as a player but, as manager of the same club, lost in the All-Ireland club championships final in 2007?

2. Who were Kerry's first All-Ireland winners?

3. The first Munster club championship was played in 1965. A Kerry team won it. Which one?

4. How many Munster titles have been won by the Kerry champions?

5. Which county has had most success at Munster level?

6. Name Kerry's most successful club at Munster championship level?

7. How many Kerry clubs have appeared in the All-Ireland club final?

8. How many have won the title?

9. Two clubs have appeared twice. Dr Croke's is one. Can you name the other?

10. Name the Kerry referee who officiated in the 1990 final between Baltinglass (Wicklow) and Clann na nGael (Roscommon).

Round

23

Captain's Log

Nothing beats walking up the steps of the Hogan Stand on All-Ireland final day to collect the cup. This round focuses on the skippers, for and against Kerry, who have had that privilege.

1. The captain of Kerry in 1986 was born in Chicago, Illinois. His time in the army earned him the nickname 'Private'. He won seven All-Irelands, nine Munster titles and three Allstars. Who is he?

2. The captain of the victorious Kerry team of 1940 later had a long career as a politician, representing a Kerry constituency in Dáil Éireann for forty years. Who was he?

3. The captain of the 1968 Down team, which defeated Kerry, went on to become the author of *Fitness for Gaelic Football* and an acknowledged authority on the rules of Gaelic football. Who was he?

4. Three members of the same family were captains of the Kerry senior footballers each year from 1960 to 1964. Who were they?

5. The captain of the Kerry 1981 All-Ireland winning team became a successful politician and government minister. Who is he?

6. Who captained Kerry to their All-Ireland final victory over Galway in millennium year, 2000?

7. The successful Kerry captain of 1969 had first appeared for Kerry seniors in 1955 at left-half forward. Who was he and in what position did he play in the 1969 final?

8. Who was the captain of the 1981 Offaly All-Ireland team which denied Kerry's bid for five-in-a-row?

9. The Kerry captain in 1997 won two U21 All-Irelands and three All-Ireland medals at senior level as well as two national leagues, an All-Ireland club championship with his club and an Allstar award. Who is he and what was his club?

10. In 1984 the GAA marked its 'Centenary year.' Who, known as 'Rosie', captained Kerry to a memorable All-Ireland final win over Dublin that year?

Walk the Line

When the team wins, they are hailed as genius, but when the team is defeated onlookers mutter that the game was 'lost on the line'. The man in the 'Bainisteoir' bib has a lot of pressure on his shoulders and this section recalls some of the managers who have walked the line for, and against, the Kingdom.

1. Kerry's 1949 All-Ireland-winning captain went on to manage the team in the late 1960s. Who was he?

2. Which Kerry manager wrote *Keys of the Kingdom*?

3. Páidí Ó Sé, in 2000, and Jack O'Connor, in 2004, managed Kerry teams that defeated Mayo in the All-Ireland finals in those years. Who was the Mayo manager on both occasions?

4. Mick O'Dwyer, Kerry's most successful manager of all time, also managed Kildare, Wicklow, Clare and which other county?

5. Which Kerry team won RTÉ's *Celebrity Bainisteoir* in 2010 when managed by Derek Burke of Crystal Swing?

6. During the twelve years Mick O'Dwyer was senior team manager, how many All-Ireland finals did Kerry appear in and how many did they win?

7. When Kerry defeated Tyrone in the 1986 All-Ireland final, who was the Tyrone manager?

8. Gerry Brown was the manager of the county that defeated Kerry in the All-Ireland final of 1968. What county did he manage?

9. Which legendary Kerryman trained or managed All-Ireland winning Kerry teams in every decade from the 1920s to the 1960s?

10. Who managed the All-Ireland-winning Kerry team of 2007?

The Writing's on the Wall

A lot has been written by, for and about Kerry football over the years. Here are the authors of ten books below. Can you match each book below with its author?

Eoghan Corry, Dick Fitzgerald, Joe O'Mahony, Mick O'Connell, Joe Ó Muircheartaigh and T.J.Flynn, Weeshie Fogarty, Richard McElligott, Jimmy O'Sullivan Darcy, Tadhg Kennelly, Sean Potts.

1. *How to Play Gaelic Football* (1914)

2. *Forging a Kingdom: The GAA in Kerry 1884–1934* (2013)

3. *Kingdom Come* (1989)

4. *Páidí: The Life of Gaelic Football Legend Páidí Ó Sé* (2001)

5. *The Kingdom: Kerry Football: The Stuff of Champions* (2010)

6. *Dr Eamonn O'Sullivan; A Man Before His Time* (2007)

7. *A Kerry Footballer* (1974)

8. *Unfinished Business* (2009)

9. *Princes in Pigskin* (2007)

10. *Forged in Green and Gold* (2009)

Round

26

Crucial Conundrums

Working out how to mark Kerry forwards, win the ball in midfield or find a way though the Kingdom defence has proved a conundrum for many years. Can you solve the Kerry conundrums below?

Players:

1. ROGER PEW (Clue: A really powerful captain!)

2. GRANNIE HALL-LACE (A show-stopper in his day)

3. PLAINEST PAL (Everyone is entitled to my opinion)

4. SOONER IMAGINED (Forever 'young')

5. LITE ONIONS (An explosive presence around 'the house')

6. A KINA HYDROGEN (Just another Kerry 'star'!)

7. HOSANNA YUMMIES (A thoroughbred 'pony')

Clubs:

8. LARGE ARSE NUN (Where's Tonto?)

9. RED ROCKS (Medicine man makes amphibian noises?)

10. DEAD PRIMROSES (Where is Derrytresk anyway?)

Penalty Points

A shrill blast of the whistle and you turn to see the referee's arms outstretched – a penalty. Joy for one team, despair for the other. Kerry have given a few, got a few, scored a few and missed a few over the years. This section relates to penalties, for and against.

1. Kerry beat Tyrone in the 1986 All-Ireland final by 2-15 to 1-10. However, in the second half when Tyrone were leading by 6 points they were awarded a penalty. Which Tyrone player opted to take a point rather than go for a goal?

2. When Kerry's Donnacha Walsh was fouled by Dublin's Stephen Cluxton in the 2013 All-Ireland semi-final, who scored from the resulting penalty?

3. Which Armagh forward missed a penalty in their 1953 All-Ireland final against Kerry?

4. Who was the Offaly goalkeeper who saved Mikey Sheehy's penalty in the 1982 All-Ireland final?

5. Which Kerry player scored twice from penalties in Kerry's 2000 Munster semi-final defeat of Cork?

6. Who had a first-half penalty saved, but later scored the only goal of the game for Kerry's opponents, in the 2002 All-Ireland final?

7. Who scored Mayo's goal from the penalty spot in their 0-13 to 1-7 loss to Kerry in the 1997 All-Ireland final?

8. In 1976, Dublin beat Kerry in the All-Ireland Final by 3-8 to 0-10. One of Dublin's goals came from a penalty. Who scored it?

9. In the 1986 All-Ireland final against Tyrone, Kerry was awarded a penalty after two minutes. Who saw his effort rebound off the crossbar?

10. In the national league game against Donegal in Ballybofey in March 2013, Michael Murphy scored a penalty goal for Donegal while in the same game a Kerry player had his penalty effort saved by Paul Durcan. Who was the Kerry player?

The Nineties

A changing of the guard took place near the end of the 1980s and with regular batches of retirements, the '90s were nothing to rave about for Kerry.

1. How many All-Ireland titles did Kerry win the 1990s?

2. Who were their opponents in the 1997 final?

3. Which county beat Kerry at the All-Ireland semi-final stage in 1991?

4. The county reached what supporters felt was an all-time low in 1992. Why?

5. Which future All-Ireland-winning captain made his championship debut that year?

6. How many championship games did Kerry play in 1993?

7. Which An Gaeltacht midfielder made his debut in 1994?

8. After four years of frustration, Kerry broke out of Munster in 1996. But which county defeated them in the All-Ireland semi-final?

9. Who was named GAA Player of the Year in 1997?

10. The curtain came down on the 1990s with defeat to Cork in that year's Munster final. Who bagged both goals for Kerry that day?

When a Star was Born

Can you match each Kerry star to the year in which he was born.

1973	1954	1951	1962	957
1969	1977	1936	1932	1983

1. Jack O'Shea.

2. John O'Keefe.

3. Mike Frank Russell.

4. Mikey Sheehy.

5. Mick O'Dwyer.

6. Seamus Moynihan.

7. Colm Cooper.

8. Maurice Fitzgerald.

9. Ambrose O'Donovan.

10. Seamus Murphy.

Round

30

Sisters are Doing it for Themselves

Women have always been equally enthusiastic when it comes to Gaelic games, but for a long time their participation was limited to supporting roles. Thankfully, that has changed and ladies' Gaelic football is one of the fastest-growing sports in Ireland. The next two sections concentrate on the ladies' game in Kerry.

1. One Kerry lady was selected for 'Team of the Decade'. Who was she?

2. Which Kerry lady scored 3-2 out of their total 4-6 when Kerry beat Offaly to win their first All-Ireland title?

3. When Kerry defeated Laois by 1-9 to 0-6 in the 1990 All-Ireland final, how many titles had they won in-a-row?

4. In 2012 Kerry appeared in their only All-Ireland final since winning in 1993 but were beaten 0-16 to 0-7. Who were their opponents?

5. Which player won a total of eight All-Irelands and six national leagues with Kerry and five county championships with her club Abbeydorney?

6. How many All-Ireland senior ladies' football titles have Kerry won?

7. On a wet and windy day in October 1982, at McDonagh Park Nenagh, Kerry won the first of their nine-in-a-row senior All-Irelands. Who were their opponents that day?

8. What is the name of the trophy awarded to the All-Ireland ladies' football winners?

9. The same two Kerry ladies won Allstars in 2012 and 2013. Name either of them.

10. The 1987 Kerry All-Ireland-winning team included Annette Walsh, Mary Lane, Bridget Leen and Margaret Flaherty all from the same club. Which club?

Kingdom Queens

Like the Kingdom men, the Kerry ladies have carried all before them on the way to provincial and national titles.

1. In what year did Kerry ladies win their first All-Ireland senior football championship?

2. Which West Kerry lady footballer played on the Kerry All-Ireland-winning team of 1993, won five Allstar awards and represented the Republic of Ireland at international level in soccer?

3. Which Castleisland man trained Kerry lady footballers to eleven All-Ireland Senior titles?

4. Which Kerry club reached the final of the All-Ireland ladies senior club championship three times, winning twice in 1980 and 1983 and being runners-up in 1986?

5. Which trophy is presented to the winners of the All-Ireland ladies senior club championship?

6. In September 2012, which county did Kerry ladies beat to reach their first senior All-Ireland final in nineteen years?

7. Mary Jo Curran won a total of ten Allstar awards. For which Kerry club did she play?

8. On 12 October 1986 for the first time, the All-Ireland senior ladies football final was played at Croke Park. Kerry ladies won by 1-11 to 0-8. Who were their opponents?

9. In 1991 Kerry's hopes of ten-in-a-row ended when they were beaten in the Munster final. Their opponents on that day went on to win the All-Ireland title that year. Who were they?

10. When Kerry won the All-Ireland title in 1993 their unfortunate opponents achieved the unenviable record of being beaten finalists for the fourth year in-a-row. Who were they?

Caman Have a Go

Kerry have led the way in Gaelic football practically since the game came into being, but the county has not enjoyed anywhere near the same success in hurling. Though it is played in pockets of the county, particularly in the north, Munster rivals Cork and Tipperary and Leinster kingpins Kilkenny are the dominant forces in the 'caman' code.

1. Kerry's first All-Ireland championship win was in hurling. When was it?

2. Who captained the side?

3. How many titles have the county won since?

4. Only club teams were allowed to enter the All-Ireland at that time. Which Kerry club brought home the honours to the Kingdom?

5. Kerry have won just one Munster minor hurling championship final. When was it?

6. How many Munster finals have Kerry contested?

7. Which Kilmoyley star won an All-Ireland senior football championship medal with the Kerry footballers in 1959 and an All-Ireland junior hurling championship with the Kingdom in 1961?

8. Dual star Tom Collins made history for playing in three Munster finals on the same day – the junior hurling final against Waterford, the junior football final, also against Waterford, and the replayed Munster senior football championship final. How many of those finals did he win?

9. Who captained Kerry to the National Hurling League Division Two title in 2001?

10. In which year did Kerry contest their only Munster hurling final at minor level?

Round

33

Hurley Burly

Although Kerry haven't enjoyed sustained success at senior level, the Kingdom's hurlers have made their mark in the second tier Christy Ring Cup that began in 2005. This section focuses on the county's exploits in that competition and on the club game in the county.

1. Who managed Kerry to their first Christy Ring Cup title in 2011?

2. Which county did they beat in the final?

3. Who top scored in every match of that successful run, including the final in which he scored 1-9?

4. On how many occasions have Kerry contested the Christy Ring Cup final?

5. Which county scored 6 goals to beat Kerry in a semi-final replay in 2009?

6. Which county beat Kerry in the 2010 final?

7. Which club has won most Kerry senior championship titles?

8. Which club won four-in-a-row between 2001 and 2004?

9. Who were Kerry's first county hurling champions?

10. Which club won the title in 1974 – sixty-one years after their previous success in 1913?

The Noughties

After the lean years of the nineties the only way was up for the Kingdom in the new nillennium. Football was changing with greater emphasis on physicality and defensive systems, but Kerry re-emerged as a force.

1. Kerry won the 2000 title after a replay. Who against?

2. In the replay win, which player opened the scoring after just seventeen seconds?

3. Who was the Kerry captain that year?

4. Which future Allstar made his debut in 2002?

5. Who were Kerry's opposition in that year's All-Ireland final?

6. Kerry were Sam Maguire winners in 2004 – but which unfashionable county forced a replay in the Munster final that year?

7. Name the Kerry manager that year?

8. He was manager again in 2006. Who did Kerry beat in that year's decider?

9. Who managed Kerry to the All-Ireland title in 2007?

10. Who was captain when Kerry won their thirty-sixth Sam Maguire in 2009?

The Warm-Down

After 340 questions, you must be exhausted. But don't stop just yet – one more section of general knowledge questions is required before this gruelling mental workout comes to an end.

1. Which club is known as the 'Naries'?

2. How many All-Ireland medals did Eoin Liston win in his career?

3. Colm Cooper scored a point in his championship debut against Limerick. In what year?

4. The following are nicknames of Gaelic players. Who is the odd one out: 'The Bomber', 'Pony', 'The Hopper'?

5. For which club does James O'Donoghue play?

6. O'Donoghue scored 3 goals as Kerry beat Tyrone 3-15 to 0-9 at Fitzgerald Stadium in March 2014. What was especially significant about the result?

7. David Moran played at midfield in that game. Who is his father?

8. Who holds Kerry's overall scoring record?

9. Where was Mick O'Connell born?

10. How many Kerry footballers were named on the GAA's 'Team of the Century'?

THE ANSWERS

Round 1 A Mixed Grill

1. Dan O'Keefe
2. Seamus Moynihan
3. 1-15 to 0-17
4. Cavan
5. Finuge
6. John O'Keefe
7. Dr Eamonn O'Sullivan
8. Pat Spillane
9. Daire O Cenneide or Tomás Ó Sé
10. Kieran Donaghy

Family Ties

1. Tom, Pat and Mick
2. Eighteen – Tom four, Pat eight, Mick six
3. 1984, 1985 and 1986
4. The Ó Sés – Darragh, Marc and Tomás
5. Mike Quirke
6. John and Tony McEntee (Armagh)
7. His brother Mike
8. Karl O'Dwyer
9. John Joe Sheehy and Sean Óg Sheehy.
   (John Joe's sons Niall and Paudie also played for Kerry)
10. Barry John Keane

AKA
(Also Known As)

1. Eoin Liston
2. Kieran Donaghy
3. The Gooch
4. It was given to him by childhood friend Peter O'Brien who said Colm bore a resemblance to a 'Goochie' doll
5. Bawn
6. Seamus Moynihan
7. Denis
8. Horse
9. Paul Galvin
10. Mike Quirke

Micko

1. Waterville
2. 1957
3. 17 points (2-11)
4. Forty-eight
5. Tipperary
6. Four
7. He began in 1975 and stepped down in 1989
8. Eight
9. Four – Kildare (two spells), Laois, Wicklow and Clare
10. Fermanagh

Grounds for Optimism

1. Austin Stack Park, Tralee and Fitzgerald Stadium, Killarney
2. Fitzgerald Stadium – capacity 43,000
3. 2009 (Qualifier v. Sligo)
4. The Polo Grounds, New York
5. Aberdorney
6. Frank Sheehy Park
7. Clonturk, Dublin
8. Thurles
9. Templenoe
10. It is named after New York-born Bob Stack who won six All-Ireland medals for Kerry

Round 6 · Páidí

1. Ventry
2. Fourteen
3. 1974–75
4. Fourteen
5. Eight
6. Offaly
7. Waterford
8. Five
9. Two (1997 and 2000)
10. Westmeath (2004)

The Swinging Sixties

1. Six
2. Down. The Mournemen became the first team from Northern Ireland to win the Sam Maguire with a 2-10 to 0-8 victory
3. Tadhgie Lyne, from the Dr Croke's club
4. Down again. This time they won 1-12 to 0-9
5. Mick O'Connell
6. Galway
7. Galway once again. The Tribesmen won three All-Ireland titles in the decade
8. Tony Barrett. He never played another championship game
9. Offaly
10. None. Kerry won 0-10 to 0-7

A League of Their Own

1. Nineteen (a record)
2. 1928
3. Kildare
4. No. Mayo won six on-the-trot between 1934 and 1939
5. Mikey Sheehy
6. New York. Kerry had won the 'home final' and then played New York in a match that ended tied at 0-12 to 0-12. The Kingdom won the replay 2-21 to 2-12
7. Kilkenny (5-20 to 1-3)
8. Kildare – by 16 points in 1958
9. A single goal, scored by Tadhgie Lyne
10. Páidí Ó Sé and Pat Spillane made their Kerry debuts

1. 1903. Kerry beat London 0-11 to 0-3
2. Thirty-six
3. Two – the 1970s and 2000s
4. It was the first final to go to a replay. Kerry beat Wexford in the second game 2-3 to 0-6
5. Pat Spillane, Mikey Sheehy, Páidí Ó Sé, Ogie Moran and Ger Power
6. Mayo in 2006
7. Kieran Donaghy, Colm Cooper and Declan O'Sullivan each scored 1-2
8. Eoin Liston
9. Two (1924: 0-4 to 0-3 v. Dublin and 1940: 0-7 to 1-3 v. Galway)
10. Jack O'Connor

1. Twenty-one
2. 1892
3. The 1990s
4. Seamus Darby of Offaly
5. Galway (1964 and 1965)
6. 9 points (1-19 to 0-13) in a replay
7. Offaly
8. It was the first time the counties had met in a championship match
9. Tadhgie Lyne (0-4)
10. Cavan

1. Seventy-five (Cork are second on thirty-seven)
2. Cork
3. 1975–82
4. It was Mick O'Dwyer's first year as manager
5. Maurice Fitzgerald (he equalled Charlie O'Sullivan's record)
6. Tipperary
7. Cork, by 11 points in 1990
8. Aodhán MacGearailt and John Crowley (both 1-3)
9. He is the only player from the Ballyduff club to have represented Kerry
10. Twenty-five years – between 1966 and 1990 they contested every final

1. 2002
2. Four
3. Two – 2006 and 2009
4. Two – 2002 and 2008
5. It was the counties' first championship meeting
6. Wicklow
7. It was Kerry's first game in the qualifiers
8. Ian Twiss
9. They beat Cork in the final after losing to the Rebels in the Munster final
10. Seamus Moynihan

Allstar State of Mind

1. Eleven
2. Donie O'Sullivan
3. Forty-nine (a record)
4. Maurice Fitzgerald
5. Connie Murphy (1989)
6. Pat Spillane
7. Nine
8. Tim's son Tadhg won an Allstar
9. 1981
10. None

The Seventies

1. Four
2. Mick O'Connell
3. 0-23 in the semi-final win against Derry
4. Offaly
5. Tony McTague
6. Pat Spillane
7. Dublin, 3-8 to 0-10
8. 17 points – 5-11 to 0-9
9. Eoin Liston
10. Dublin once again

Round 15 — Far Off Fields

1. Mikey Sheehy
2. Mick Galway
3. Moss Keane
4. Queen's Park Rangers
5. Sydney Swans
6. Sean Wight
7. Dick Spring
8. Tommy Walsh
9. Eoin Liston
10. Kieran Donaghy

1. Mike McAuliffe
2. Clare
3. Mick O'Dwyer
4. Daniel 'Danno' O'Keefe
5. Ger Power
6. Mike Frank Russell
7. Paudie Lynch
8. Pat, Tom and Mike Spillane
9. Mick O'Connell and Jack O'Shea
10. David O'Callaghan

Who's Who?

1. Tomás Ó Sé
2. Dick Fitzgerald
3. Sean Kelly
4. Mikey Sheehy
5. Seamus Moynihan
6. Pat Spillane
7. Paul Russell
8. Páidí Ó Sé
9. Tommy Sugrue
10. Eoin Liston

Who, What, Where, When, Why ... ?

1. They both saved a penalty in an All-Ireland final:
   Furlong in 1982 *v.* Kerry, O'Keefe 2002 *v.* Armagh
2. John Bannon , Longford
3. Three (2004, 2006 and 2009)
4. Colm Cooper
5. London
6. 1929
7. O'Connor – twenty-two
8. Kerry refused to travel
9. Eugene Magee
10. They were sent off in an All-Ireland final

19 Numbers Game

1. 56
2. 4
3. 75
4. 9
5. 6
6. 7
7. 8
8. 36
9. 14
10. 10

Rogue number: 23

A Set of Clubs

1. Listowel Emmet's
2. Laune Rangers
3. Dr Croke's
4. They were all Spillanes, Pat, Mick, Tom, Jerome and Tom senior (father of Pat, Tom and Mick)
5. An Ghaeltacht
6. Austin Stack's
7. Tralee Mitchel's
8. St Senan's
9. Dromid Pearse's
10. Killorglin

The Eighties

1. Three
2. Roscommon, in a game that ended 1-9 to 1-6 in Kerry's favour
3. Eight – it finished 4-15 to 4-10
4. Offaly
5. Seamus Darby of Offaly
6. Wexford – 1915, 1916, 1917, 1918
7. Cromane
8. Seán O'Sullivan
9. Ambrose O'Donovan
10. Tyrone

Clubbing Together

1. Pat O'Shea (Dr Croke's)
2. East Kerry (1971)
3. Shannon Rangers
4. Thirteen
5. Cork (twenty-six titles)
6. Dr Croke's – six titles
7. Eight
8. Five – East Kerry (1971), Austin Stack's (1977), Castleisland Desmond's (1985), Dr Croke's (1992) and Laune Rangers (1996)
9. Castleisland Desmond's won the competition in 1985 and were runners-up the following year
10. Tommy Sugrue

Captain's Log

1. Tommy Doyle
2. Dan Spring
3. Joe Lennon
4. Paudie, Sean Óg and Niall Sheehy
5. Jimmy Deenihan
6. Seamus Moynihan
7. Johnny Culloty – goalkeeper
8. Richie Connor
9. Liam Hassett, Laune Rangers
10. Ambrose O'Donovan

Walk the Line

1. Jackie Lyne
2. Jack O'Connor
3. John Maughan
4. Laois (2003 – 2006)
5. Castleisland Desmonds
6. Ten appearances – eight wins
7. Art McRory
8. Down
9. Dr Eamonn O'Sullivan
10. Pat O'Shea

1. Dick Fitzgerald
2. Richard McElligott
3. Eoghan Corry
4. Sean Potts
5. Joe O'Mahony
6. Weeshie Fogarty
7. Mick O'Connell
8. Tadhg Kennelly
9. Joe Ó Muirceartaigh and T.J. Flynn
10. Jimmy O'Sullivan Darcy

Crucial Conundrums

1. Ger Power
2. Charlie Nelligan
3. Pat Spillane
4. Denis 'Ogie' Moran
5. Eoin Liston
6. Kieran Donaghy
7. Seamus Moynihan
8. Laune Rangers
9. Dr Croke's
10. Dromid Pearses

Round 27 — Penalty Points

1. Kevin McCabe
2. James O'Donoghue
3. Bill McCorry
4. Martin Furlong
5. Daire O'Cinneide
6. Oisín McConville
7. Ciaran McDonnell
8. Jimmy Keaveney
9. Jack O'Shea
10. Kieran O'Leary

The Nineties

1. One
2. Mayo – Kerry ended an eleven-year dry spell with victory
3. Down, on their way to the title
4. Kerry lost to Clare in the Munster final
5. Seamus Moynihan
6. One – losing to Cork in the Munster semi-final was the end of the road
7. Darragh Ó Sé
8. Mayo
9. Maurice Fitzgerald
10. Aodhán MacGearailt (An Gaeltacht)

When a Star was Born

1. 1957
2. 1951
3. 1977
4. 1954
5. 1936
6. 1973
7. 1983
8. 1969
9. 1962
10. 1932

Sisters are Doing it for Themselves

1. Geraldine O'Shea
2. Mary Geaney
3. Nine
4. Cork
5. Anne Costelloe
6. Eleven
7. Offaly
8. The Brendan Martin Cup
9. Sarah Houlihan or Louise Muircheartaigh
10. Castleisland

Kingdom Queens

1. 1976
2. Geraldine O'Shea
3. Mick Fitzgerald
4. Castleisland
5. The Dolores Tyrrell Memorial Cup
6. Galway
7. Beaufort
8. Wexford
9. Waterford
10. Laois

Caman Have a Go

1. 1891
2. John Mahoney
3. None
4. Kilmoyley, a team from north Kerry, disbanded and joined up with Ballyduff so that their joint team could win the All-Ireland
5. 1891
6. Five (winning 1891, losing in 1899, 1890, 1892 and 1908)
7. Tom Collins
8. Two. Kerry lost the Munster football final to Cork 1–8 to 1–7
9. Michael Slattery
10. 1938 (they lost to Cork, whose team included the legendary Christy Ring)

Hurley Burly

1. John Meyler
2. Wicklow – 2-21 to 2-8
3. Darragh O'Connell
4. Three
5. Carlow
6. Westmeath
7. Ballyduff
8. Kilmoyley
9. Kenmare (1889)
10. Abbeydorney

The Noughties

1. Galway
2. Johnny Crowley
3. Seamus Moynihan
4. Colm Cooper
5. Armagh
6. Limerick
7. Jack O'Connor
8. Mayo
9. Pat O'Shea
10. Darran O'Sullivan

The Warm-Down

1. Kerrins O'Rahilly's
2. Seven
3. 2002
4. The Hopper – Michael McGrath, Galway Hurler is the odd one out. The other two are Kerry footballers – Seamus 'Pony' Moynihan and Eoin 'Bomber' Liston)
5. Killarney Legion
6. It was biggest defeat Tyrone had suffered under Mickey Harte's management
7. Denis 'Ogie' Moran
8. Mikey Sheehy (51-456 – a total of 609 points)
9. Valentia Island
10. Six – Dan O'Keefe, Sean Murphy, Mick O'Connell, Jack O'Shea, Pat Spillane and Mikey Sheehy